H‌ **rs**

Lu‌ ng

**d the
t for
ality**

D0335521

Sarah Ridley

W

This edition 2013

First published in 2009 by
Franklin Watts
338 Euston Road
London NW1 3BH

Franklin Watts Australia
Level 17/207 Kent Street
Sydney NSW 2000

Copyright © Franklin Watts 2009

Series Editor: Jeremy Smith
Art Director: Jonathan Hair
Design: Simon Morse
Cover Design: Jonathan Hair
Picture Research: Sarah Ridley

Picture credits: AFP/Getty Images:
front cover, 1, 2. AP/Topfoto: 18, 21.
Bettmann/Corbis: 7, 12, 13, 15, 16, 17, 19,
22. Marjory Collins/Bettmann/
Corbis: 6. Raymond Gehman/Corbis:
10. Marvin Koner/Corbis: 14. Bob
Krist/Corbis: 5. Popperfoto/Getty
Images: 20. Flip Schulke/Corbis: 8.
Donald Uhrbrock/Time Life/Getty
Images: 9. Eudora Welty/Corbis: 11.

Every attempt has been made to clear
copyright. Should there be any
inadvertent omission please apply to
the publisher for rectification.

Dewey classification: 323.1'196'073'092
ISBN: 978 1 4451 1793 5

A CIP catalogue record for this book is
available from the British Library

Franklin Watts is a division of
Hachette Children's Books, an
Hachette UK company.
www.hachette.co.uk

Printed in China

Contents

The King family

On the 15th January 1929, the Reverend King and his wife had a son. They named him Michael but changed his name to Martin Luther a few years later.

1927 ▶

Willie, Martin's sister, is born.

15 January
1929 ▶

Michael (later Martin Luther) King is born.

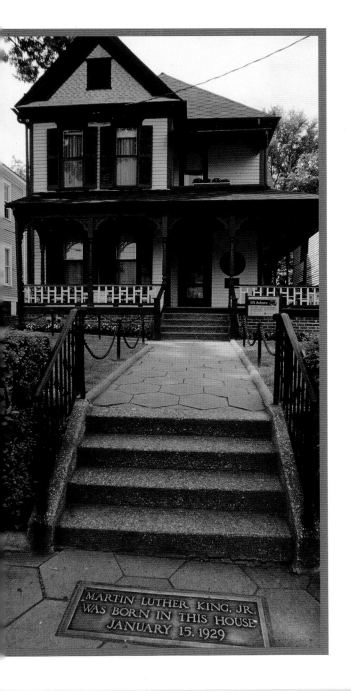

The family lived in a comfortable house in the city of Atlanta in the south of the United States of America (USA).

The house where Martin Luther King grew up.

To school

As a young boy, Martin played with white and black children. But when it was time to start school, the black children went to one school and the white to another.

A school for black children. Usually, these schools were not as good as those for white children.

1935

Martin starts school.

White and black (coloured) people had different public drinking fountains.

FOR COLORED ONLY

Gradually, Martin realised that black and white people were treated differently in his country. Black people even had to sit apart from white people on the bus and use different public toilets.

1939 ▶

The Second World War begins in Europe.

The student

Martin was clever and he did well at school. He went to college and university, where he learnt how to be a church minister, like his father.

▶ As a student and later on, Martin gave sermons at his father's church.

1944 ▶

Martin goes to Morehouse College in Atlanta, Georgia.

1945 ▶

The Second World War ends.

During his time at Boston University he met a young music student called Coretta Scott. They fell in love and were married.

Coretta played the piano. This photo shows her with Martin and two of their children in 1960.

1947 ▶

Martin studies at Crozer Theological Seminary, Pennsylvania.

1951 ▶

Martin goes to Boston University.

1953 ▶

Martin marries Coretta.

Return to the south

At the age of 25, Martin took the job of pastor at a church in Montgomery in the south of the USA. A year later, Coretta and Martin had their first baby.

◀ Martin was the pastor of this church in Montgomery, USA.

May
1954 ▶

By law, black and white children should be using the same schools but many white people stop that from happening.

In the south of the USA, life was much harder for black people than in the north. Martin saw that black people had the worst houses, schools and jobs. They were treated differently from white people in many areas of life.

▲ Black Americans had to use the coloured entrance at the cinema.

Rosa Parks

In December 1955, Martin heard about the arrest of a black woman called Rosa Parks. The Montgomery police arrested her when she refused to give up her bus seat to a white person.

▶ Rosa Parks did not see why she should give up her seat to a white person.

December
1955 ▶

Rosa Parks is arrested.

1955-1956 ▶

The bus protest in Montgomery.

Martin was arrested for his part in the bus protest. Here he walks out of court with Coretta.

The black people of Montgomery asked Martin to lead a protest to show how angry they felt. They stopped using the buses. After a year, the bus company said that black people could sit wherever they liked.

1956 ▶

A bomb is thrown at Martin's home. No one is injured.

1957 ▶

The Kings' second child, Martin Luther King III, is born.

13

Protest

In 1959, Martin gave up his church job and joined others to fight for equal rights for all black Americans. He gave speeches, wrote books, led marches and organised protests.

◀ Despite all this hard work, Martin loved spending time with his children.

Martin is stabbed in a bookshop.

Martin steps down from his job as pastor.

Martin believed that all protest should be peaceful, even after someone threw a bomb at his house, and another stabbed him. His strong belief in God continued to shine through in his speeches.

Martin's speeches inspired people to join the struggle for fair treatment of black Americans.

1960 ▶

The King family moves to Atlanta, Georgia.

1961 ▶

The Kings' third child, Dexter, is born.

Birmingham

Birmingham was a city where black Americans were treated very badly. Martin organised marches to protest at their treatment — and thousands joined him.

Martin was often arrested at protest marches, and went to jail 13 times in all.

1962 ▶

Martin joins the Birmingham protests.

Police ordered firemen to turn hoses on the peaceful protestors at Birmingham, Alabama.

When newspaper photos showed police and firemen attacking the protestors, even more people realised how badly black people were treated in some parts of the USA.

1963 ▶

The Kings' fourth child, Bernice, is born.

'I have a dream'

More and more people wanted to see black Americans treated fairly. When Martin organised a march in Washington D.C. in 1963, 250,000 people came along.

Martin waves to the crowd at the Washington D.C. march.

August
1963 ▶

Huge march in Washington D.C., the capital of the USA.

Martin made his most famous speech at the march. Here is some of it:

'I have a dream that my four little children will one day live in a nation where they will not be judged by the colour of their skin but by the content of their character.'

US President Kennedy is shot dead.

Success at last

The following year, the US government finally made a law that gave equal rights to all Americans. Black people should now be treated the same as white people in all areas of life.

▲ Martin continued to lead marches and protests to improve the lives of black Americans.

July 1964 ▶	December 1964 ▶	1965 ▶
Civil Rights Act becomes law.	Martin receives the Nobel Peace Prize.	Vietnam War begins.

That same year, Martin won the Nobel Peace Prize. This prize is given out each year to the person who is seen to have done the most for peace in the world.

▶ Martin and his Nobel Peace Prize.

1965 ▶

Martin speaks at a huge march in Selma, Alabama, USA.

1965 ▶

Voting Rights Act makes it clear that all people should have the vote.

21

Death

Sadly, many people did not want to see the changes Martin and others worked towards. In April 1968, Martin was shot by one of these people and died soon afterwards.

◀ This photo shows Martin and some friends standing on the same hotel balcony where he was shot.

January
1966 ▶
Martin moves to Chicago.

May
1966 ▶
Martin speaks out against the Vietnam War.

Crowds follow Martin Luther King's coffin through the streets of Atlanta.

Thousands joined the King family at the funeral. Americans continue to remember his life on Martin Luther King Day, a public holiday in January.

4 April
1968 ▶

Martin Luther King is shot dead.

1986 ▶

Martin Luther King Day becomes a public holiday.

Glossary

Equal rights The same rights for everyone, regardless of their wealth or the colour of their skin. Equal rights aim to give people the same chances in life.

Minister/Pastor/Reverend All names for clergymen. They are the people who lead church services and look after the religious needs of the people who live in the area surrounding the church.

Second World War (1939-45) A world war.

Sermon The part of a church service when the minister or pastor gives a religious speech.

Vietnam War (1965-1973) The US army fought an unsuccessful war in Vietnam. Thousands died.

Vote The right to vote in elections.

Index